MAGNA CARTA

1 King John's effigy in Worcester Cathedral

MAGNA CARTA

G. R. C. DAVIS

THE BRITISH LIBRARY

© 1977, The British Library Board
First published 1963
Reprint (revised) 1965
Second Reprint (revised) 1971
Third Reprint (revised) 1977
Fourth Reprint (revised) 1982
Fifth Reprint 1985
Sixth Reprint 1989
Seventh Reprint 1992
Eighth Reprint 1994
Ninth Reprint 1996
Tenth Reprint 1997
Eleventh Reprint 1998
Twelfth Reprint 1999

British Library Cataloguing in Publication Data
British Library
Magna Carta
I. Magna Carta
I. Title   II. Davis, G. R. C.
942.033   JN147
ISBN 0712300147

Printed in Great Britain
by Henry Ling Ltd, Dorchester, Dorset

PREFACE

THIS booklet sets out to explain to the general reader the background of the Magna Carta documents exhibited in the British Library and to answer the questions about them most commonly asked by visitors.

The present revised reprint—the sixth since the original publication in 1963—is substantially unchanged from its predecessors, but the bibliography has been brought up to date and some other minor changes made.

CONTENTS

PLATES

Map to show Places mentioned in the Text

I

THE MAKING OF
MAGNA CARTA

MAGNA CARTA, the Great Charter of English liberties, was first issued by King John at Runnymede in June 1215. Immediately after John's death in October 1216, it was reissued in the name of his successor, Henry III, with substantial excisions and alterations. Two subsequent reissues in 1217 and 1225 incorporated further revisions. In the form of the third and final revision of 1225, it was confirmed in 1297 by Edward I and a copy of this confirmation was afterwards placed on the first or 'great' roll of English statutes.

Since then, Magna Carta has come to be regarded by Englishmen, and by all who have adopted English laws, as their chief constitutional defence against arbitrary or unjust rule. Its two most famous clauses (§§ 39 & 40) express and give warranty to some of the Englishman's most deeply held political beliefs. Translated from the original Latin they read:

> No free man shall be seized or imprisoned, or stripped of his rights or possessions, or outlawed or exiled, or deprived of his standing in any other way, nor will we proceed with force against him, or send others to do so, except by the lawful judgement of his equals or by the law of the land.
> To no one will we sell, to no one deny or delay right or justice.

In these and other clauses, seventeenth-century lawyers were to find a basis for such fundamental English privileges and rights as trial by jury, Habeas Corpus, equality before the law, freedom from arbitrary arrest, and parliamentary control of taxation. For such reasons Magna Carta could be described by William Pitt, earl of Chatham, in 1770 as forming, with the Petition of Right (1629) and the Bill of Rights (1689), the 'Bible of the English Constitution'.

In the form of its first issue by King John, Magna Carta represents a treaty of peace imposed upon him by barons who had rebelled against him for reasons that the charter's terms themselves make clear. His financial

9

demands in aid of his foreign wars were held to be oppressive; the methods by which taxation was assessed and collected were arbitrary and extortionate; reprisals against defaulters were ruthless and brutal; for wrongs suffered there was no redress. For these abuses a remedy was sought, and since it was by charters that medieval kings customarily made their most solemn and binding grants to their subjects, it was through a charter that men thought that an effective remedy might be found.

About the events that led up to the first issue of Magna Carta—later identified by the lawyers as 'The Charter of Runnymede'—few firm facts are known. The evidence on this point of the actual documents of the charter, and of other contemporary records, although indisputably authentic, is fragmentary. The more connected narratives offered by the monastic chroniclers—chief amongst them Roger of Wendover, a contemporary monk of St Albans—are often of questionable reliability. Many gaps in the evidence can be filled only by conjecture, and no account of what took place can claim to be entirely satisfactory.

According to Roger of Wendover, the proposal to secure a charter of liberties from King John was first put forward in the late summer of 1213. John had then occupied the throne for more than fourteen years, and faced by conspiracy at home to bring about his overthrow, and the threat of invasion from abroad by the French king, Philip Augustus, had for some time been negotiating to regain the support of the Church. This support he had forfeited in 1207 by his defiance of Pope Innocent III in refusing to accept Stephen Langton as archbishop of Canterbury, and as a result England had since 1208 lain under papal interdict, by which no service might be held in any church, and he himself had since 1209 been in a state of excommunication. Now, however, a reconciliation was being effected. He had agreed to accept Langton as archbishop, to reinstate the clergy who had gone into exile on account of the interdict, and to compensate the Church for the lands and revenues that he had taken from it in reprisal. On 15 May 1213, at Temple Ewell near Dover, he had resigned to the Pope his kingdoms of England and Ireland, receiving them back under a vassal's bonds of fealty and homage, and for an annual tribute to the Holy See of 1,000 marks (about £666). In July, at Winchester, he had been absolved from excommunication by the newly-returned Langton, and had reaffirmed his coronation oath, with added promises to maintain the ancient laws of the realm, ascribed traditionally to Edward the Confessor. Still to be accomplished, but by this time scarcely more than formalities, remained the final ratification of the surrender of his kingdoms, to be made at St Paul's Cathedral, London, on 3 October 1213, its formal acceptance by the Pope on 21 April 1214, at Rome, and the raising of the interdict in the following July. By transforming himself in this way from a spiritual outcast into a liege-man of the Pope, he had won important new sources of support. The opposition to him was divided, and the balance of power

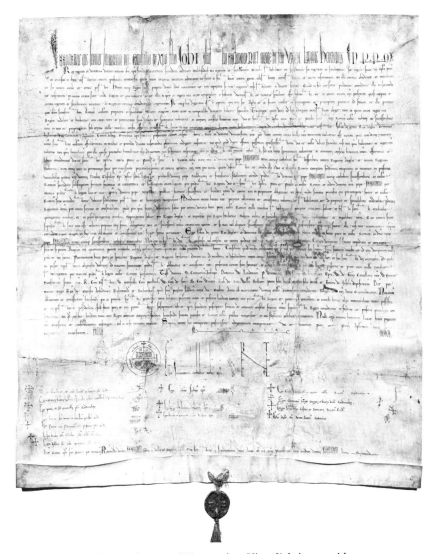

2 *Bull of Pope Innocent III accepting King John's vassaldom, 1214*
actual size: 23¾ × 27½ in.

had been tilted at least temporarily in his favour.

But despite the verbal promises that John had given at Winchester in July, and that had been repeated in his name by Geoffrey Fitz Peter, the chief justice, at a council held at St Albans on 4 August 1213 to discuss the restoration to the Church of its forfeited possessions, his honesty of purpose remained in doubt. More specific guarantees about his future conduct were sought. At a further council held at St Paul's Cathedral on 25 August, Langton, who seems quickly to have assumed the position of a

3   Silver penny of King John struck in Ireland (twice actual size)

political leader traditionally held by archbishops of Canterbury at this period, is said to have proposed that the King should be asked to confirm or reissue the charter of liberties granted by Henry I at his coronation in 1100, in which undertakings had been given of the type that were now required. The proposal was greeted with acclaim, and all present swore solemn oaths that when the opportune moment arose, they would fight to the death to secure such a charter.

Immediate progress towards this aim was frustrated by the preparations and departure of John for a new campaign in France. These were accompanied by fresh demands for men and money that excited further unrest, especially in the north of England, where the opposition to him was fiercest. It was consequently not until his return in October 1214, after a disastrous conclusion to his venture, that matters could be carried firmly forward. While he was staying at the Temple, in London, in January 1215, a party of barons appeared before him, arrayed in full armour, and presented the demands—by this time more elaborately conceived—for a charter that should confirm the ancient liberties of the kingdom, as set out in Edward the Confessor's laws, in the coronation charter of Henry I, and in the coronation oath renewed by John himself, eighteen months beforehand.

To these demands John succeeded, with some difficulty, in deferring an answer to a meeting at Northampton on the Sunday after Easter—26 April—on the grounds that the matter was too complex for immediate reply. Meanwhile he at once despatched envoys to Rome, to apprise his overlord, the Pope, of the situation. He also began to marshal his resources for a trial of strength. Among other preparatory measures, on 4 March he took the Cross as a crusader, a step that secured for his person and his possessions the Church's most special protection.

In Holy Week 1215, ten days before the date appointed by John for the

12

delivery of his answer, the malcontent barons came together at Stamford, in Lincolnshire, and made their way southwards to Northampton and Brackley. At Brackley, since John had not appeared at Northampton, they repeated in writing, and apparently in more forceful and specific terms, the demands that they had made in January, delivering them to the King's representatives, including Langton and William Marshal, earl of Pembroke, who had come there to meet them.

In this form the renewed demands appear to have been brought to the King at Wallingford, almost at the same time as the Pope's replies to the letters sent to Rome in January. These enjoined both parties to the dispute to exercise moderation, preferring negotiation to force, and put forward proposals for a peaceful settlement, of which the precise terms are unknown but that were probably for some kind of arbitration. The Pope's proposal John offered to accept, but he rejected those of the barons as tantamount to the surrender of his kingdoms. At this the barons, unwilling to protract negotiations further, renounced their loyalty and obedience to him. They appointed Robert Fitz Walter, lord of Dunmow, in Essex, as their general, with the title of 'Marshal of the Army of God and of the Holy Church', and laid siege to the nearest royal castle at Northampton.

On 9 May, John formally proposed to the barons the establishment of a court of arbitration, consisting of representatives of either party and the Pope. On the following day, he further undertook that, until such arbitration had taken place, he 'would not take them or their men, or deprive them of their possessions, nor go against them by force or with arms, except by the law of his realm or by the judgement of their equals in his court'. The appearance in this undertaking of phrases that were to reappear five weeks later in the actual text of Magna Carta perhaps indicates how far the situation had by this time developed. His proposals, however, were rejected, and the barons' capture of London on 17 May increased decisively the strength of their position. A renewal of the proposals on 29 May was again refused.

At the same time as this open exchange and rejection of offers, less conspicuous negotiations seem to have been taking place, in which Langton and William Marshal, earl of Pembroke, continued to act as two of the principal intermediaries. To the influence of these intermediaries should probably be attributed the transformation of Magna Carta from a mere settlement of baronial grievances into the document of much more far-reaching significance that it was, in the event, to become. At what stage it became possible to begin to argue and draft a list of heads of agreement is uncertain, but at latest by 10 June the parties had been successfully brought together in conference at Runnymede, a field conveniently situated beside the River Thames between the royal castle of Windsor, and a baronial camp at Staines. By 15 June the list had been completed, and could be laid before the King there for his formal acceptance and seal.

4 *The Articles of the Barons sealed by King John at Runnymede, 1215
actual size: $10\frac{1}{2} \times 21\frac{3}{4}$ in.*

While its basis remained the charter of Henry I, of which renewal had originally been sought, its terms had by now been greatly amplified and enlarged so as to command the support of a much larger field of interests.

The document containing this list, which bears no date, is now preserved in the British Library. It consists of a strip of parchment, the normal writing material of the period, $21\frac{3}{4}$ inches long and $10\frac{1}{2}$ inches wide, to which John's seal was originally attached by a second strip of parchment threaded through a fold at the foot. Although the seal appears to have remained attached in this way until the nineteenth century, it has since broken away from the document, and is exhibited beside it. The document itself is commonly known as 'The Articles of the Barons' from the heading, which reads (in Latin) 'These are the articles (*capitula*) that the barons seek and the King concedes'. Its contents itemise 49 points that form the basis of Magna Carta. The crux of the terms lies in the final clauses, which arranged for the establishment of a council of twenty-five barons to superintend the charter's enforcement. This overrode completely any vestige of authority that John might still consider himself to possess. His consent to it best indicates the desperate nature of the position into which he had been driven.

With the sealing of the Articles of the Barons, Magna Carta had virtually been brought into being, and the date that it bears (15 June) may well be that on which this sealing took place. From negotiation, matters passed into the hands of the legal draftsmen and the secretariat of the royal chancery, where the heads of agreement were amplified into the conventional form of a charter, and one or two further clauses, such as the first one of all, guaranteeing the freedom of the Church, were added. The way was opened to the restoration, four days later, of 'firm and reformed peace', the ceremonial re-rendering of homage and fealty to the King, and the return to the barons of their forfeited lands, castles, and hostages. Eight days after the Articles had been sealed, on 23 June, the meeting at Runnymede broke up, and the charter itself may be presumed to have attained its final shape. Written exemplifications of it are known to have been in existence on the following day, to be sent out to those who required them. The basis of their distribution is uncertain, but it has been plausibly suggested by Professor C. R. Cheney that acquisition of them was dependent, as with other royal grants, upon payment of the prescribed fees. Sheriffs of counties and bishops are referred to by contemporary chroniclers as being among those who received them, but the issue is actually recorded of only thirteen of them, three of which were handed to two bishops, and ten to the steward of the archbishop of Canterbury for onward transmission. Of the four such exemplifications that survive, two are now in the archives of the Deans and Chapters of Lincoln and Salisbury, to which they were consigned for safe-keeping by their original recipients—either the bishops or the sheriffs—at latest by the fourteenth century. Of the two others, now

5   The Seal of King John placed on the Articles of the Barons
obverse and (right) reverse
actual diameter: $3\frac{3}{4}$ in.

both preserved in the British Library, one seems originally to have been sent to the Barons of the Cinque Ports at Dover and the destination of the second is unknown. No two of the four are of exactly the same size or shape: they are written by different hands, and there are slight variations in the texts, consisting mainly of transpositions of words and discrepancies of spelling. This suggests that the master text from which they were copied was in a rough and much corrected state, so that it was difficult to transcribe accurately.

The spirit in which Magna Carta was finally accepted by King John can only be surmised. Mistrust of his intentions towards it are implicit in the guarantees and securities that it imposed upon him, and although for a month or two he paid it lip-service, it is improbable that he regarded acquiescence in it as more than a temporary expedient. In defiance of the undertaking given by him in the charter that he would not seek to have it set aside by any outside authority (§ 61), he seems at once to have sent further envoys to the Pope, and before it could be made fully effective messengers had returned, perhaps by the end of September, bringing ·solemn bulls, dated at Rome on 24 and 25 August, in the first of which Innocent III declared the whole compact to be null and void because the King had been compelled to enter upon it by force and fear. The charter itself was stated to be 'as unlawful and unjust as it is base and shameful . . . whereby the Apostolic See is brought into contempt, the

royal prerogative diminished, the English outraged, and the whole enterprise of the Crusade gravely imperilled.'

At this, civil war, which had continued to smoulder despite the restoration of 'firm peace', broke out once more in full force. At the end of September, Langton set off for Rome to attend the fourth Lateran Council and on arrival there was suspended from office for his failure to carry out the Pope's orders against the King's adversaries. Early next year, Louis, son of the French king, Philip Augustus, came over to England to join forces with the rebels as a pretender to the throne in John's place. The aim of the opposition to John was no longer to secure agreement with him, but to achieve his destruction. The Charter of Runnymede seemed likely to pass into the limbo of forgotten things, had not John died unexpectedly in October 1216, at the age of 49, from dysentery brought on, as it was said, by a surfeit of peaches and new cider. He died at Newark, and was buried in Worcester Cathedral.

With the accession to the throne of John's son Henry III, aged nine, Magna Carta was at once revived by the young king's supporters, and hastily converted from an instrument for the suppression of tyranny into a manifesto by which men of moderate views might be rallied to his cause. On 12 November 1216, a fortnight after Henry III's coronation at Gloucester, it was reissued at Bristol, substantially revised and re-edited to meet the altered circumstances of the new reign, and on this occasion with

6   *Exemplification of King Henry III's reissue of Magna Carta, 1225*
actual size: $12\frac{1}{4} \times 19\frac{1}{2}$ *in*

papal support. In the autumn of the following year, 1217, it was again re-issued with still further revision after the conclusion of a peace treaty with the now routed Louis, and his withdrawal to France. On this and sub-sequent occasions the clauses dealing with the law of the royal forests were made the subject of separate charters, known as 'Charters of the Forest', and Magna Carta itself began to be so styled by the lawyers, for purposes of distinction. Eight years later, in 1225, Magna Carta was reissued for a third time with smaller and, as events were to prove, final revisions, in return for the concession to the King of the right to levy a special tax on movable goods.

In the form of the 1225 revision—of which the Lacock Abbey exempli-fication, sent originally to the sheriff of Wiltshire, is preserved in the British Library—Magna Carta was confirmed or reissued on three further oc-casions by Henry III in the course of his long reign (in 1237, 1253, and 1265) and again by Edward I in 1297 as evidence of good intentions. It was in the form of Edward I's confirmation of 12 October 1297, eighty-two years after its first issue at Runnymede, that a copy of it was later placed on the Statute Roll. Although confirmed on many subsequent occasions by later kings, it is at this point that the history of the making of Magna Carta may be said effectively to end.

7 *Exemplification of* ...
actual si...

n's Magna Carta, 1215
×13½ in

II

THE TEXT OF
MAGNA CARTA
1215

INTRODUCTORY NOTE

As might be expected, the text of the Magna Carta of 1215 bears many traces of haste, and is clearly the product of much bargaining and many hands. Most of its clauses deal with specific, and often long-standing, grievances rather than with general principles of law. Some of the grievances are self-explanatory: others can be understood only in the context of the feudal society in which they arose. Of a few clauses, the precise meaning is still a matter of argument.

In feudal society, the king's barons held their lands 'in fee' (*feudum*) from the king, for an oath to him of loyalty and obedience, and with the obligation to provide him with a fixed number of knights whenever these were required for military service. At first the barons provided the knights by dividing their estates (of which the largest and most important were known as 'honours') into smaller parcels described as 'knights' fees', which they distributed to tenants able to serve as knights. But by the time of King John it had become more convenient and usual for the obligation for service to be commuted for a cash payment known as 'scutage', and for the revenue so obtained to be used to maintain paid armies.

Besides military service, feudal custom allowed the king to make certain other exactions from his barons. In times of emergency, and on such special occasions as the marriage of his eldest daughter, he could demand from them a financial levy known as an 'aid' (*auxilium*). When a baron died, he could demand a succession duty or 'relief' (*relevium*) from the baron's heir. If there was no heir, or if the succession was disputed, the baron's lands could be forfeited or 'escheated' to the Crown. If the heir was under age, the king could assume the guardianship of his estates, and enjoy all the profits from them—even to the extent of despoliation—until the heir came of age. The king had the right, if he chose, to sell such a guardianship to the highest bidder, and to sell the heir himself in marriage for such price as the value of his estates would command. The widows and daughters of barons might also be sold in marriage. With their own tenants, the barons could deal similarly.

The scope for extortion and abuse in this system, if it were not benevolently applied, was obviously great and had been the subject of complaint long before King John came to the throne. Abuses were, moreover, aggravated by the difficulty of obtaining redress for them, and in Magna Carta the provision of the means for obtaining a fair hearing of complaints, not only against the king and his agents but against lesser feudal lords, achieves corresponding importance.

About two-thirds of the clauses of the Magna Carta of 1215 are concerned with matters such as these, and with the misuse of their powers by royal officials. As regards other topics, the first clause, conceding the freedom of the Church, and in particular confirming its right to elect its own dignitaries without royal interference, reflects John's dispute with the Pope over Stephen Langton's election as archbishop of Canterbury (see p. 10): it does not appear in the Articles of the Barons, and its somewhat stilted phrasing seems in part to be attempting to justify its inclusion, none the less, in the charter itself. The clauses that deal with the royal forests (§§ 44, 47, 48), over which the king had special powers and jurisdiction, reflect the disquiet and anxieties that had arisen on account of a long-standing royal tendency to extend the forest boundaries, to the detriment of the holders of the lands affected. Those that deal with debts (§§ 9–11) reflect administrative problems created by the chronic scarcity of ready cash among the upper and middle classes, and their need to resort to money-lenders when this was required. The clause promising the removal of fish-weirs (§ 33) was intended to facilitate the navigation of rivers. A number of clauses deal with the special circumstances that surrounded the making of the charter, and are such as might be found in any treaty of peace. Others, such as those relating to the city of London (§ 13) and to merchants (§ 41), clearly represent concessions to special interests.

TRANSLATION

(Clauses marked (†) are still valid under the charter of 1225, but with a few minor amendments. Clauses marked (*) were omitted in all later reissues of the charter. In the charter itself the clauses are not numbered, and the text reads continuously. The translation sets out to convey the sense rather than the precise wording of the original Latin.)

JOHN, by the grace of God King of England, Lord of Ireland, Duke of Normandy and Aquitaine, and Count of Anjou, to his archbishops, bishops, abbots, earls, barons, justices, foresters, sheriffs, stewards, servants, and to all his officials and loyal subjects, Greeting.

KNOW THAT BEFORE GOD, for the health of our soul and those of our ancestors and heirs, to the honour of God, the exaltation of the holy

Church, and the better ordering of our kingdom, at the advice of our reverend fathers Stephen, archbishop of Canterbury, primate of all England, and cardinal of the holy Roman Church, Henry archbishop of Dublin, William bishop of London, Peter bishop of Winchester, Jocelin bishop of Bath and Glastonbury, Hugh bishop of Lincoln, Walter Bishop of Worcester, William bishop of Coventry, Benedict bishop of Rochester, Master Pandulf subdeacon and member of the papal household, Brother Aymeric master of the knighthood of the Temple in England, William Marshal earl of Pembroke, William earl of Salisbury, William earl of Warren, William earl of Arundel, Alan de Galloway constable of Scotland, Warin Fitz Gerald, Peter Fitz Herbert, Hubert de Burgh seneschal of Poitou, Hugh de Neville, Matthew Fitz Herbert, Thomas Basset, Alan Basset, Philip Daubeny, Robert de Roppeley, John Marshal, John Fitz Hugh, and other loyal subjects:

†(1) FIRST, THAT WE HAVE GRANTED TO GOD, and by this present charter have confirmed for us and our heirs in perpetuity, that the English Church shall be free, and shall have its rights undiminished, and its liberties unimpaired. That we wish this so to be observed, appears from the fact that of our own free will, before the outbreak of the present dispute between us and our barons, we granted and confirmed by charter the freedom of the Church's elections—a right reckoned to be of the greatest necessity and importance to it—and caused this to be confirmed by Pope Innocent III. This freedom we shall observe ourselves, and desire to be observed in good faith by our heirs in perpetuity.

To ALL FREE MEN OF OUR KINGDOM we have also granted, for us and our heirs for ever, all the liberties written out below, to have and to keep for them and their heirs, of us and our heirs:

(2) If any earl, baron, or other person that holds lands directly of the Crown, for military service, shall die, and at his death his heir shall be of full age and owe a 'relief', the heir shall have his inheritance on payment of the ancient scale of 'relief'. That is to say, the heir or heirs of an earl shall pay £100 for the entire earl's barony, the heir or heirs of a knight 100s. at most for the entire knight's 'fee', and any man that owes less shall pay less, in accordance with the ancient usage of 'fees'.

(3) But if the heir of such a person is under age and a ward, when he comes of age he shall have his inheritance without 'relief' or fine.

(4) The guardian of the land of an heir who is under age shall take from it only reasonable revenues, customary dues, and feudal services. He shall do this without destruction or damage to men or property. If we have given the guardianship of the land to a sheriff, or to any person answerable to us for the revenues, and he commits destruction or damage, we will exact compensation from him, and the land shall be entrusted to two

worthy and prudent men of the same 'fee', who shall be answerable to us for the revenues, or to the person to whom we have assigned them. If we have given or sold to anyone the guardianship of such land, and he causes destruction or damage, he shall lose the guardianship of it, and it shall be handed over to two worthy and prudent men of the same 'fee', who shall be similarly answerable to us.

(5) For so long as a guardian has guardianship of such land, he shall maintain the houses, parks, fish preserves, ponds, mills, and everything else pertaining to it, from the revenues of the land itself. When the heir comes of age, he shall restore the whole land to him, stocked with plough teams and such implements of husbandry as the season demands and the revenues from the land can reasonably bear.

(6) Heirs may be given in marriage, but not to someone of lower social standing. Before a marriage takes place, it shall be made known to the heir's next-of-kin.

(7) At her husband's death, a widow may have her marriage portion and inheritance at once and without trouble. She shall pay nothing for her dower, marriage portion, or any inheritance that she and her husband held jointly on the day of his death. She may remain in her husband's house for forty days after his death, and within this period her dower shall be assigned to her.

(8) No widow shall be compelled to marry, so long as she wishes to remain without a husband. But she must give security that she will not marry without royal consent, if she holds her lands of the Crown, or without the consent of whatever other lord she may hold them of.

(9) Neither we nor our officials will seize any land or rent in payment of a debt, so long as the debtor has movable goods sufficient to discharge the debt. A debtor's sureties shall not be distrained upon so long as the debtor himself can discharge his debt. If, for lack of means, the debtor is unable to discharge his debt, his sureties shall be answerable for it. If they so desire, they may have the debtor's lands and rents until they have received satisfaction for the debt that they paid for him, unless the debtor can show that he has settled his obligations to them.

*(10) If anyone who has borrowed a sum of money from Jews dies before the debt has been repaid, his heir shall pay no interest on the debt for so long as he remains under age, irrespective of whom he holds his lands. If such a debt falls into the hands of the Crown, it will take nothing except the principal sum specified in the bond.

*(11) If a man dies owing money to Jews, his wife may have her dower and pay nothing towards the debt from it. If he leaves children that are under age, their needs may also be provided for on a scale appropriate to the size of his holding of lands. The debt is to be paid out of the residue,

reserving the service due to his feudal lords. Debts owed to persons other than Jews are to be dealt with similarly.

*(12) No 'scutage' or 'aid' may be levied in our kingdom without its general consent, unless it is for the ransom of our person, to make our eldest son a knight, and (once) to marry our eldest daughter. For these purposes only a reasonable 'aid' may be levied. 'Aids' from the city of London are to be treated similarly.

†(13) The city of London shall enjoy all its ancient liberties and free customs, both by land and by water. We also will and grant that all other cities, boroughs, towns, and ports shall enjoy all their liberties and free customs.

*(14) To obtain the general consent of the realm for the assessment of an 'aid'—except in the three cases specified above—or a 'scutage', we will cause the archbishops, bishops, abbots, earls, and greater barons to be summoned individually by letter. To those who hold lands directly of us we will cause a general summons to be issued, through the sheriffs and other officials, to come together on a fixed day (of which at least forty days notice shall be given) and at a fixed place. In all letters of summons, the cause of the summons will be stated. When a summons has been issued, the business appointed for the day shall go forward in accordance with the resolution of those present, even if not all those who were summoned have appeared.

*(15) In future we will allow no one to levy an 'aid' from his free men, except to ransom his person, to make his eldest son a knight, and (once) to marry his eldest daughter. For these purposes only a reasonable 'aid' may be levied.

(16) No man shall be forced to perform more service for a knight's 'fee', or other free holding of land, than is due from it.

(17) Ordinary lawsuits shall not follow the royal court around, but shall be held in a fixed place.

(18) Inquests of *novel disseisin, mort d'ancestor,* and *darrein presentment* shall be taken only in their proper county court. We ourselves, or in our absence abroad our chief justice, will send two justices to each county four times a year, and these justices, with four knights of the county elected by the county itself, shall hold the assizes in the county court, on the day and in the place where the court meets.

(19) If any assizes cannot be taken on the day of the county court, as many knights and freeholders shall afterwards remain behind, of those who have attended the court, as will suffice for the administration of justice, having regard to the volume of business to be done.

(20) For a trivial offence, a free man shall be fined only in proportion to the degree of his offence, and for a serious offence correspondingly, but not so heavily as to deprive him of his livelihood. In the same way, a merchant shall be spared his merchandise, and a husbandman the implements of his husbandry, if they fall upon the mercy of a royal court. None of these fines shall be imposed except by the assessment on oath of reputable men of the neighbourhood.

(21) Earls and barons shall be fined only by their equals, and in proportion to the gravity of their offence.

(22) A fine imposed upon the lay property of a clerk in holy orders shall be assessed upon the same principles, without reference to the value of his ecclesiastical benefice.

(23) No town or person shall be forced to build bridges over rivers except those with an ancient obligation to do so.

(24) No sheriff, constable, coroners, or other royal officials are to hold lawsuits that should be held by the royal justices.

*(25) Every county, hundred, wapentake, and tithing shall remain at its ancient rent, without increase, except the royal demesne manors.

(26) If at the death of a man who holds a lay 'fee' of the Crown, a sheriff or royal official produces royal letters patent of summons for a debt due to the Crown, it shall be lawful for them to seize and list movable goods found in the lay 'fee' of the dead man to the value of the debt, as assessed by worthy men. Nothing shall be removed until the whole debt is paid, when the residue shall be given over to the executors to carry out the dead man's will. If no debt is due to the Crown, all the movable goods shall be regarded as the property of the dead man, except the reasonable shares of his wife and children.

*(27) If a free man dies intestate, his movable goods are to be distributed by his next-of-kin and friends, under the supervision of the Church. The rights of his debtors are to be preserved.

(28) No constable or other royal official shall take corn or other movable goods from any man without immediate payment, unless the seller voluntarily offers postponement of this.

(29) No constable may compel a knight to pay money for castle-guard if the knight is willing to undertake the guard in person, or with reasonable excuse to supply some other fit man to do it. A knight taken or sent on military service shall be excused from castle-guard for the period of this service.

(30) No sheriff, royal official, or other person shall take horses or carts for transport from any free man, without his consent.

(31) Neither we nor any royal official will take wood for our castle, or for any other purpose, without the consent of the owner.

(32) We will not keep the lands of people convicted of felony in our hand for longer than a year and a day, after which they shall be returned to the lords of the 'fees' concerned.

(33) All fish-weirs shall be removed from the Thames, the Medway, and throughout the whole of England, except on the sea coast.

(34) The writ called *precipe* shall not in future be issued to anyone in respect of any holding of land, if a free man could thereby be deprived of the right of trial in his own lord's court.

(35) There shall be standard measures of wine, ale, and corn (the London quarter), throughout the kingdom. There shall also be a standard width of dyed cloth, russett, and haberject, namely two ells within the selvedges. Weights are to be standardised similarly.

(36) In future nothing shall be paid or accepted for the issue of a writ of inquisition of life or limbs. It shall be given *gratis*, and not refused.

(37) If a man holds land of the Crown by 'fee-farm', 'socage', or 'burgage', and also holds land of someone else for knight's service, we will not have guardianship of his heir, nor of the land that belongs to the other person's 'fee', by virtue of the 'fee-farm', 'socage', or 'burgage', unless the 'fee-farm' owes knight's service. We will not have the guardianship of a man's heir, or of land that he holds of someone else, by reason of any small property that he may hold of the Crown for a service of knives, arrows, or the like.

(38) In future no official shall place a man on trial upon his own unsupported statement, without producing credible witnesses to the truth of it.

†(39) No free man shall be seized or imprisoned, or stripped of his rights or possessions, or outlawed or exiled, or deprived of his standing in any other way, nor will we proceed with force against him, or send others to do so, except by the lawful judgement of his equals or by the law of the land.

†(40) To no one will we sell, to no one deny or delay right or justice.

(41) All merchants may enter or leave England unharmed and without fear, and may stay or travel within it, by land or water, for purposes of trade, free from all illegal exactions, in accordance with ancient and lawful customs. This, however, does not apply in time of war to merchants from a country that is at war with us. Any such merchants found in our country at the outbreak of war shall be detained without injury to their persons or property, until we or our chief justice have discovered how our own merchants are being treated in the country at war with us. If our own merchants are safe they shall be safe too.

*(42) In future it shall be lawful for any man to leave and return to our kingdom unharmed and without fear, by land or water, preserving his allegiance to us, except in time of war, for some short period, for the common benefit of the realm. People that have been imprisoned or outlawed in accordance with the law of the land, people from a country that is at war with us, and merchants—who shall be dealt with as stated above—are excepted from this provision.

(43) If a man holds lands of any 'escheat' such as the 'honour' of Wallingford, Nottingham, Boulogne, Lancaster, or of other 'escheats' in our hand that are baronies, at his death his heir shall give us only the 'relief' and service that he would have made to the baron, had the barony been in the baron's hand. We will hold the 'escheat' in the same manner as the baron held it.

(44) People who live outside the forest need not in future appear before the royal justices of the forest in answer to general summonses, unless they are actually involved in proceedings or are sureties for someone who has been seized for a forest offence.

*(45) We will appoint as justices, constables, sheriffs, or other officials, only men that know the law of the realm and are minded to keep it well.

(46) All barons who have founded abbeys, and have charters of English kings or ancient tenure as evidence of this, may have guardianship of them when there is no abbot, as is their due.

(47) All forests that have been created in our reign shall at once be disafforested. River-banks that have been enclosed in our reign shall be treated similarly.

*(48) All evil customs relating to forests and warrens, foresters, warreners, sheriffs and their servants, or river-banks and their wardens, are at once to be investigated in every county by twelve sworn knights of the county, and within forty days of their enquiry the evil customs are to be abolished completely and irrevocably. But we, or our chief justice if we are not in England, are first to be informed.

*(49) We will at once return all hostages and charters delivered up to us by Englishmen as security for peace or for loyal service.

*(50) We will remove completely from their offices the kinsmen of Gerard de Athée, and in future they shall hold no offices in England. The people in question are Engelard de Cigogné, Peter, Guy, and Andrew de Chanceaux, Guy de Cigogné, Geoffrey de Martigny and his brothers, Philip Marc and his brothers, with Geoffrey his nephew, and all their followers.

*(51) As soon as peace is restored, we will remove from the kingdom all the foreign knights, bowmen, their attendants, and the mercenaries that have come to it, to its harm, with horses and arms.

*(52) To any man whom we have deprived or dispossessed of lands, castles, liberties, or rights, without the lawful judgement of his equals, we will at once restore these. In cases of dispute the matter shall be resolved by the judgement of the twenty-five barons referred to below in the clause for securing the peace (§ 61). In cases, however, where a man was deprived or dispossessed of something without the lawful judgement of his equals by our father King Henry or our brother King Richard, and it remains in our hands or is held by others under our warranty, we shall have respite for the period commonly allowed to Crusaders, unless a lawsuit had been begun, or an enquiry had been made at our order, before we took the Cross as a Crusader. On our return from the Crusade, or if we abandon it, we will at once render justice in full.

*(53) We shall have similar respite in rendering justice in connexion with forests that are to be disafforested, or to remain forests, when these were first afforested by our father Henry or our brother Richard; with the guardianship of lands in another person's 'fee', when we have hitherto had this by virtue of a 'fee' held of us for knight's service by a third party; and with abbeys founded in another person's 'fee', in which the lord of the 'fee' claims to own a right. On our return from the Crusade, or if we abandon it, we will at once do full justice to complaints about these matters.

(54) No one shall be arrested or imprisoned on the appeal of a woman for the death of any person except her husband.

*(55) All fines that have been given to us unjustly and against the law of the land, and all fines that we have exacted unjustly, shall be entirely remitted or the matter decided by a majority judgement of the twenty-five barons referred to below in the clause for securing the peace (§ 61) together with Stephen, archbishop of Canterbury, if he can be present, and such others as he wishes to bring with him. If the archbishop cannot be present, proceedings shall continue without him, provided that if any of the twenty-five barons has been involved in a similar suit himself, his judgement shall be set aside, and someone else chosen and sworn in his place, as a substitute for the single occasion, by the rest of the twenty-five.

(56) If we have deprived or dispossessed any Welshmen of lands, liberties, or anything else in England or in Wales, without the lawful judgement of their equals, these are at once to be returned to them. A dispute on this point shall be determined in the Marches by the judgement of equals. English law shall apply to holdings of land in England, Welsh law to those in Wales, and the law of the Marches to those in the Marches. The Welsh shall treat us and ours in the same way.

*(57) In cases where a Welshman was deprived or dispossessed of any-

thing, without the lawful judgement of his equals, by our father King Henry or our brother King Richard, and it remains in our hands or is held by others under our warranty, we shall have respite for the period commonly allowed to Crusaders, unless a lawsuit had been begun, or an enquiry had been made at our order, before we took the Cross as a Crusader. But on our return from the Crusade, or if we abandon it, we will at once do full justice according to the laws of Wales and the said regions.

*(58) We will at once return the son of Llywelyn, all Welsh hostages, and the charters delivered to us as security for the peace.

*(59) With regard to the return of the sisters and hostages of Alexander, king of Scotland, his liberties and his rights, we will treat him in the same way as our other barons of England, unless it appears from the charters that we hold from his father William, formerly king of Scotland, that he should be treated otherwise. This matter shall be resolved by the judgement of his equals in our court.

(60) All these customs and liberties that we have granted shall be observed in our kingdom in so far as concerns our own relations with our subjects. Let all men of our kingdom, whether clergy or laymen, observe them similarly in their relations with their own men.

*(61) Since we have granted all these things for God, for the better ordering of our kingdom, and to allay the discord that has arisen between us and our barons, and since we desire that they shall be enjoyed in their entirety, with lasting strength, for ever, we give and grant to the barons the following security:

The barons shall elect twenty-five of their number to keep, and cause to be observed with all their might, the peace and liberties granted and confirmed to them by this charter.

If we, our chief justice, our officials, or any of our servants offend in any respect against any man, or transgress any of the articles of the peace or of this security, and the offence is made known to four of the said twenty-five barons, they shall come to us—or in our absence from the kingdom to the chief justice —to declare it and claim immediate redress. If we, or in our absence a broad the chief justice, make no redress within forty days, reckoning from the day on which the offence was declared to us or to him, the four barons shall refer the matter to the rest of the twenty-five barons, who may distrain upon and assail us in every way possible, with the support of the whole community of the land, by seizing our castles, lands, possessions, or anything else saving only our own person and those of the queen and our children, until they have secured such redress as they have determined upon. Having secured the redress, they may then resume their normal obedience to us.

Any man who so desires may take an oath to obey the commands of the twenty-five barons for the achievement of these ends, and to join with them in assailing us to the utmost of his power. We give public and free permission to take this oath to any man who so desires, and at no time will we prohibit any man from taking it. Indeed, we will compel any of our subjects who are unwilling to take it to swear it at our command.

If one of the twenty-five barons dies or leaves the country, or is prevented in any other way from discharging his duties, the rest of them shall choose another baron in his place, at their discretion, who shall be duly sworn in as they were.

In the event of disagreement among the twenty-five barons on any matter referred to them for decision, the verdict of the majority present shall have the same validity as a unanimous verdict of the whole twenty-five, whether these were all present or some of those summoned were unwilling or unable to appear.

The twenty-five barons shall swear to obey all the above articles faithfully, and shall cause them to be obeyed by others to the best of their power.

We will not seek to procure from anyone, either by our own efforts or those of a third party, anything by which any part of these concessions or liberties might be revoked or diminished. Should such a thing be procured, it shall be null and void and we will at no time make use of it, either ourselves or through a third party.

*(62) We have remitted and pardoned fully to all men any ill-will, hurt, or grudges that have arisen between us and our subjects, whether clergy or laymen, since the beginning of the dispute. We have in addition remitted fully, and for our own part have also pardoned, to all clergy and laymen any offences committed as a result of the said dispute between Easter in the sixteenth year of our reign (*i.e.* 1215) and the restoration of peace.

In addition we have caused letters patent to be made for the barons, bearing witness to this security and to the concessions set out above, over the seals of Stephen archbishop of Canterbury, Henry archbishop of Dublin, the other bishops named above, and Master Pandulf.

*(63) IT IS ACCORDINGLY OUR WISH AND COMMAND that the English Church shall be free, and that men in our kingdom shall have and keep all these liberties, rights, and concessions, well and peaceably in their fulness and entirety for them and their heirs, of us and our heirs, in all things and all places for ever.

Both we and the barons have sworn that all this shall be observed in good faith and without deceit. Witness the abovementioned people and many others.

Given by our hand in the meadow that is called Runnymede, between Windsor and Staines, on the fifteenth day of June in the seventeenth year of our reign (*i.e.* 1215: *the new regnal year began on 28 May*).

III

THE DOCUMENTS OF
MAGNA CARTA
exhibited in the British Library

1. BULL OF POPE INNOCENT III, dated at St. Peter's, Rome, 21 April 1214, accepting King John's resignation to the Roman Church of his kingdoms of England and Ireland. In return he takes the king, his heirs, and the two realms under the protection of St Peter and himself, granting the realms back to John and his successors in fee, on condition that they swear an oath of fealty to him at their accession.

In its text, the bull recites the letters sealed by John with a seal of gold at St Paul's Cathedral, London, on 3 October 1213, in which he acknowledged that he had made this surrender to obtain remission of his sins, had performed liege homage to the papal legate. and had bound his successors to do the same, paying an annual tribute to the Holy See of 1,000 marks (about £666)—700 marks in respect of England, and 300 for Ireland.

At the end of the text, the bull is attested by Innocent III's *signum* or motto in a roundel, 'Fac mecum, Domine, signum in bonum', taken from Psalm 85, to which he has added in his own hand the cross at the head. This is followed by his name, before which he has himself written the initial 'E' of 'Ego', by a notarial mark of authentication 'SS' (for 'subscripsi'), and by the monogram 'Bene valete'. Beneath these are the attestations of three cardinal bishops and eleven other cardinals, in which all the crosses, and parts of the inscriptions, are autograph. Across the bottom is the date of issue. From the foot, the Pope's leaden seal or *bulla* is appended by a silk cord.

An earlier bull, dated 4 November 1213, that accepts similarly John's first act of surrender at Dover on 15 May, is also in the British Library (*Cotton MS. Cleopatra* E.1, f.149) but not exhibited. Both bulls were originally kept in the Treasury of the Exchequer, and passed into the hands of Sir Robert Cotton in the early 17th century. With the rest of his library they came to the British Museum at its foundation in 1753 and thus to the British Library in 1973.

Plate 2   *Cotton Charter* VIII. 24

2. THE ARTICLES OF THE BARONS: the original document submitted to King John at Runnymede, as the basis of Magna Carta, and sealed there probably on 15 June 1215. The heading of the document, which is undated, reads 'Ista sunt capitula quae Barones petunt et dominus Rex concedit' ('These are the articles that the Barons seek and the Lord King concedes'). The articles or clauses are forty-nine in number, and were expanded in Magna Carta itself to sixty-three. The colour of the ink in articles 26–32 and 45–47 (corresponding to §§ 36–42, 12, 58, 59, and 47 respectively of Magna Carta as printed in translation on pp. 15–25) is lighter than that of the rest, suggesting that these may have been added at a comparatively late stage in the drafting. The King's seal, of white wax, originally hung from the foot of the document by a parchment tag, but became separated from it in the nineteenth century.

The document is shown by a thirteenth-century inventory to have been kept in the archives of the archbishops of Canterbury at St Gregory's Priory, Canterbury, not many years after its execution, and was presumably taken from Runnymede and placed there for safety by Stephen Langton. It is said to have been removed, with other papers, from Lambeth Palace—the archbishops' London residence—by John Warner, bishop of Rochester, after Archbishop Laud's impeachment in 1640. It came later into the hands of Gilbert Burnet, bishop of Salisbury, who died in 1715, and passed from his daughter Mary, or her husband David Mitchell, into the possession of Philip, Earl Stanhope, who presented it to the British Museum in 1769.

Plates 4 and 5   *Additional MS.* 4838

3 & 4. EXEMPLIFICATIONS OF KING JOHN'S MAGNA CARTA, 1215: two of the exemplifications of the text of Magna Carta that were received by bishops, sheriffs, and others, on and after 23 June 1215, over King John's seal. Two other exemplifications survive in the archives of Lincoln and Salisbury Cathedrals. All four are dated 15 June 1215, the date on which the Articles of the Barons are thought to have been sealed at Runnymede, but differ slightly in size, shape, and text. Only No. 4 below still retains any trace of the King's seal. A translation of the text is given on pp. 23–33.

3. The original destination of this is unknown. A note on the back states that it was given to Sir Robert Cotton by Humphrey Wyems or Wymes, of the Inner Temple, on 1 January 1629. According to one account, it had been found in a London tailor's shop. The three slits at the foot appear to have been made at a later date and are not connected with the seal, which is now lost. The few short passages and words that have been written after the end of the main text are, in the Lincoln and Salisbury exemplifications, incorporated into the main body of it. They may consequently represent last-minute revisions, made after engrossment had begun.

Plate 7   *Cotton MS. Augustus* II. 106

4. This was sent to Sir Robert Cotton by Sir Edward Dering, in 1630, from Dover Castle, where it had apparently been found amongst the records. It is presumably the exemplification that is known from other sources to have been sent to the Barons of the Cinque Ports on or after 24 June 1215. It was badly damaged by fire on 23 October 1731, when the Cotton Library was housed at Ashburnham House, Westminster, and is now virtually illegible. Early facsimiles show that it contained more numerous additions at the end than No. 3. The seal was reduced by the fire to a lump of shapeless wax.

Cotton Charter XIII. 31a

5. BULL OF POPE INNOCENT III condemning and annulling Magna Carta, dated at Anagni, 24 August 1215. The bull recites in Latin the circumstances of John's quarrel with the Pope, his surrender of his kingdoms to the Church, and his dispute with the barons, 'so that by force and fear, that might have assailed even the most courageous of men, he was impelled to enter into an agreement with them as unlawful and unjust as it was base and shameful, to the excessive diminution of his own right and honour'. It continues: 'We, not wishing to close our eyes to such audacious wickedness, whereby the Apostolic See is brought into contempt, the royal prerogative diminished, the English nation outraged, and the whole enterprise of the Crusade gravely imperilled . . . do utterly reprobate and condemn this agreement, and under ban of anathema we command that neither the King shall presume to observe it, nor the barons and their accomplices to require its observation; utterly cancelling and making void both the charter itself and any pledges or obligations that may have been made in any way concerning it, so that neither now nor hereafter shall they be of any validity'.

The Pope's leaden *bulla* is attached to the foot by silk cords. Like No. 1, the bull was originally kept in the Treasury of the Exchequer, and passed into the hands of Sir Robert Cotton in the early seventeenth century.

Cotton MS. Cleopatra E. 1, ff. 155–156

6. EXEMPLIFICATION OF HENRY III'S REISSUE OF MAGNA CARTA, 1225: the third revision of the original Magna Carta of King John, issued by Henry III on 11 February 1225. After several further reissues and confirmations by Henry III and Edward I, the text came eventually to be enrolled on the first or 'great' roll of the Statutes, probably in the reign of Edward I, and represents the charter's final form.

Among other alterations, this reissue of Magna Carta omits entirely the following clauses that appeared in the charter of 1215. Those dealing with the royal forests were transferred to a separate Forest Charter in 1217, and the remainder disappeared. The numeration is that used in the translation of the charter of 1215 printed on pp. 23-33:

§§ 10, 11, 12, 14, 15, 25, 27, 42, 45, 48-53, 55, 57, 58, 59, 61-63.

Nine new clauses and a new conclusion were added, to give a total, after some rearrangement, of forty-seven clauses.

According to Matthew Paris, exemplifications of the charter of 1225 were sent to every county but, as in the case of the 1215 charter, the accuracy of this statement by a contemporary chronicler is unconfirmed. The Library's copy is that obtained by the county of Wiltshire and was deposited at Lacock Abbey for safe-keeping, apparently by the abbey's foundress, and later abbess, Ela, widow of William Longespée, earl of Salisbury, who had been sheriff when it was received. It remained at Lacock until presented to the British Museum in 1945 by Miss Matilda Talbot, C.B.E. Other exemplifications of this issue of Magna Carta survive in the archives of Durham Cathedral and of the Duchy of Lancaster, the latter being exhibited in the Public Record Office Museum, Chancery Lane.

Plate 6   *Additional MS.* 46144

The British Library has a number of exemplifications of later confirmations and reissues of Magna Carta, but these are not shown. Exemplifications of Edward I's confirmation of 12 October 1297, the version that was subsequently placed on the Statute Roll, are preserved among the records of the City of London in the Guildhall, at the National Library of Australia, Canberra (MS.1508, formerly at Bruton School, Somerset), and among the records of the Duchy of Lancaster. A fourth exemplification is in private hands. The Duchy of Lancaster charter, together with the enrolment on the Statute Roll, is exhibited in the Public Record Office Museum.

FURTHER READING

THE most recent comprehensive study of Magna Carta is J. C. Holt's *Magna Carta*, Cambridge, 1969, in which the Latin texts of the Articles of the Barons, the 1215 charter (with English translation), the 1225 charter and other relevant documents are printed, with a full bibliography. A fully revised edition, with a legal commentary, is due to be published in 1990.

The Latin texts of the principal English documents are printed by W. Stubbs, *Select Charters and other Illustrations of English Constitutional History*, 9th edition revised by H. W. C. Davis, Oxford, 1921, and C. Bémont, *Chartes des libertés anglaises*, Paris, 1892. The texts of the two bulls of Innocent III are printed, with English translations, by C. R. Cheney and W. H. Semple, *Selected Letters of Pope Innocent III*, Edinburgh, 1953.

For the chronology of events in June 1215 I have followed C. R. Cheney, 'The Eve of Magna Carta', *Bulletin of the John Rylands Library*, xxxviii, 1955–56, pp. 311–41. His article 'The Twenty Five Barons of Magna Carta', *ibid.*, l, 1967–68, pp. 280–307, should also be noted. Both were reprinted, with other relevant essays, in Professor Cheney's *The Papacy and England 12th–14th Centuries*, Variorum Reprints, 1982. V. H. Galbraith, 'A draft of Magna Carta (1215)', *Proceedings of the British Academy*, liii, 1967, pp. 345–60 (reprinted in his *Kings and Chronicles*, Hambledon, 1982), also discusses the sequence of events. An alternative chronology to Professor Cheney's is proposed by Professor Holt, 'The Making of Magna Carta', *English Historical Review*, lxxii, 1957, pp. 401–22, and adopted by him in his book. His article, 'A vernacular Text of Magna Carta', *ibid.*, lxxxix, 1974, pp. 346–64, discusses a significant discovery bearing on the contemporary publication of Magna Carta. These and other Magna Carta essays by Professor Holt are collected in his *Magna Carta and Medieval Government*, Hambledon, 1985.

There are good general articles on Magna Carta by Doris M. Stenton in the *Encyclopaedia Britannica*, 1970, and Chambers's Encyclopaedia, 1966. Her classic *English Society in the Early Middle Ages*, 3rd edn., 1962, is valuable for the wider historical background, which is also well described by A. L. Poole, *From Domesday Book to Magna Carta*, 2nd edn. 1955, and W. L. Warren, *King John*, 1961 (paperback reprint, 1966); and, more recently, by M. T. Clanchy, *England and its Rulers 1066–1272*, Fontana, 1983.

The photograph of King John's effigy in Worcester Cathedral (cover) is reproduced by courtesy of Nicholas Servian (Woodmansterne Ltd.); and the frontispiece by courtesy of the National Buildings Record.

I am indebted to Professor C. R. Cheney, Dr P. D. A. Harvey, and a number of colleagues in the British Library Department of Manuscripts for valuable advice and criticism on many points of detail.